WILLIAM PENN

17th Century Founding Father

Selections from His Political Writings

EDWIN B. BRONNER

Pendle Hill Pamphlet 204

About the Author/The relationship of Edwin Bronner to Quakerism is a close one. Librarian, Curator of the Quaker Collection, and Professor of History at Haverford College, he is also a former member of Pendle Hill's board of directors and has served as Chairman of the Friends World Committee for Consultation since January, 1974. He is President of the Friends Historical Association in America, and a past President of the Friends Historical Society in London. Of his many publications dealing with the Society of Friends the most recent is *"The Other Branch:" London Yearly Meeting and the Hicksites, 1827-1912.*

But it is his special knowledge of the great Founder of Pennsylvania which concerns us here. For as author of *William Penn's "Holy Experiment"* and many articles on the subject he is a member of the "Committee on the Papers of William Penn," which has supervised the collection and cataloging of all manuscripts in order to microfilm them and make them available to libraries. He is currently at work on the definitive list of Penn's printed works which is being prepared at Haverford. The present pamphlet contains selections from the Founder's political writings, accompanied by helpful comment and a concise biographical introduction.

ISBN 0-87574-204-1
Library of Congress catalog card number 75-32728

Printed in the United States of America by
Sowers Printing Company, Lebanon, Pennsylvania

November 1975: 3,000

Introduction: Penn's Life and Achievements

At a time Americans are looking at their history and paying tribute to the Founding Fathers who contributed so much to the beginnings of our nation two hundred years ago, it is timely to call attention to another Founding Father who was active a century earlier.

William Penn is honored as one of the founders of three of the thirteen original states: New Jersey, Pennsylvania, and Delaware. He is remembered for his plan for a union of the American colonies proposed nearly sixty years before Benjamin Franklin's Albany Plan was introduced. Furthermore, Penn holds a permanent place in American history as a leading advocate of religious toleration, civil liberty and representative government.

His reputation does not, however, rest exclusively upon these important contributions to the creation of the American nation. *An Essay Towards the Present and Future Peace of Europe,* published in 1693, assures Penn recognition as a man of vision. His plan for an international organization to preserve peace is remembered along with those advocated by Grotius and Sully in the seventeenth century. In addition, Penn's ideas about education, prison reform, race relations, city planning, and respect for the natural world (ecology), were ahead of his time.

Imprisoned several times during his early years as a Quaker, Penn had a deep concern for those who violated the law. He made a special effort to provide justice for those accused of crimes when he drew up the laws for Pennsylvania. He insisted that fines be moderate, and that they be consistent with the severity of the offense. Most important, in place of the English criminal code, which listed some 200 capital offenses, he limited the death penalty to only two, murder and treason. He substituted imprisonment at hard labor for execution, and emphasized the importance of reforming prisoners during their incarceration, rather than the idea of punishment.

The most familiar image of William Penn is the one showing him making a treaty with the Lenni Lenape Indians under the great elm tree on the banks of the Delaware at Shackamaxon. Even though this event cannot be authenticated, it symbolizes the fact that Penn treated the aborigines as brothers and as equals. He not only paid a just price for the land, he made provision for equal justice before the law, and gained the admiration and respect of the Native Americans.

William Penn advocated practical education of children in place of the classical pattern prevalent in his day, adding that the emphasis upon memorization, theoretical knowledge, words and rules, left "their natural genius to mechanical and physical, or natural knowledge uncultivated and neglected." In Pennsylvania he made provision for schools where all children would learn to read and write and prepare for some trade, "that the poor may work to live, and the rich, if they become poor may not want." He actively supported the founding of the school known today as William Penn Charter School, which dates from 1689.

Like many other Friends, Penn was closely in tune with nature, and advocated living near to the soil. He said, "it were happy if we studied nature more in natural things, and acted according to nature, whose rules are few, plain, and most reasonable. . . . The country is both the philosopher's garden and his library, in which he reads and contemplates the power, wisdom and goodness of God."

He created Philadelphia as a planned city, with streets running east and west between the Delaware and Schuylkill rivers, crossed by streets running north and south. He provided for a large open square in the center, and four smaller squares, in each quarter of the area. He urged the settlers to build their houses on relatively large plots of land with ample gardens around them. George B. Tatum, in *Penn's Great Town* (Philadelphia, 1961) wrote, "modern city planners might fairly claim William Penn as among the first to practice their profession in the New World."

❧

William Penn was born in London in 1644 during one of the most troubled periods of English history. Parliament and a substantial portion of the people were waging Civil War against the King, Charles I. Penn's father, also named William, was an important naval figure on the side of Parliament during the war, and was rewarded with fame and property for his contribution to victory over the Crown. Admiral Penn later became involved in a serious disagreement with Oliver Cromwell, the leader of the Commonwealth government, as it was called, and changed his allegiance to the King in exile, Charles II. When the latter was restored to the throne of England in 1660, he rewarded the men who had helped him regain power, including Admiral Penn. A close relationship between the royal family and the Penns continued for the next half century, as long as the Stuarts were on the English throne.

The Admiral and his wife, Margaret Jasper van de Schuren Penn, both owned estates in Ireland. Thus, when Admiral Penn and Cromwell quarreled, it seemed logical for the family to go into semi-retirement in Ireland. There young William Penn continued his education with the aid of private tutors; earlier he had studied at Chigwell School, outside of London. In 1660, the year of the Restoration of Charles II, he was ready, at the age of sixteen, to enter Oxford University.

While at Oxford young Penn became involved with a nonconformist group, and eventually found himself in conflict with university authorities. Expelled from Christ Church, his college at Oxford, for his religious beliefs, he spent two years on the continent of Europe, including an extended period of time studying at the Huguenot university at Saumur in the Loire valley. After his return to England in 1664, he studied law for a time at Lincoln's Inn, and was back once more in Ireland, supervising his father's estates, when he made the final decision to embrace the Quaker movement in 1667.

As a member of the small and despised religious sect, Penn was persecuted and imprisoned in an era when religious toleration was virtually unknown. He began to work for religious toleration in England, and later established religious freedom in his new colony of Pennsylvania. During this time he first wrote *No Cross, No Crown* (revised and enlarged in 1682), which has gone through more than fifty editions, including translations into several foreign languages. When he was tried, in 1670, along with William Mead, on charges growing out of holding religious services in the streets, Penn, and the jury which heard the case, resisted the pressure of the presiding judge. In the appeals which followed, the precedent was established that juries may not be intimidated by judges.

During the next decade the young convert made two visits to the Dutch and German states to visit Quakers and to engage in religious ministry. Because he had studied in Lincoln's Inn, one of the Inns of Court where Englishmen prepared for the legal profession, Penn was chosen in 1675 to attempt to settle a dispute between two Quakers over control of West New Jersey. Eventually he became involved in the government of both East and West New Jersey. In addition, he made an important contribution to the defense of political liberty in England while supporting the campaigns of Algernon Sidney, a radical candidate for a seat in the House of Commons. In these campaigns

Penn made speeches and published political tracts defending the fundamental rights of Englishmen, and insisting that they should have proper elected representation in the government.

In 1681 the Crown granted him the province known as Pennsylvania. Charles II, who owed the estate of his former admiral the sum of £16,000, used this means to settle the debt, and insisted that the colony should be named for his old friend. The new proprietor, after making as many preparations for the founding of the province as was possible from the eastern shore of the Atlantic, set sail for the New World in the summer of 1682. He arrived in the Delaware Bay in the ship *Welcome* in late October, and spent two years in the colony before returning to England. During his stay in Pennsylvania, Penn agreed to revise the First Frame of government, as well as the laws agreed upon in England. He guaranteed religious toleration to all, made agreements with the Indians, and took great satisfaction in the prosperous manner in which the province began to develop.

Penn spent the next fifteen years back in England. During the first five of these years he reached great heights as a personal friend and advisor of James II, but suffered the ignominy of imprisonment and suspicion after the Glorious Revolution of 1688. He even lost control of Pennsylvania for two years. However it was during this period that he published two of his most famous works, the *Essay Towards . . . the Peace of Europe,* and *Fruits of Solitude.* After 1694 his fortunes began to rise once more, and in 1699 he returned to Pennsylvania for two years. Toward the close of this second visit Penn granted the settlers the Charter of Privileges of 1701 which remained the constitution of Pennsylvania until 1776, and made some additional suggestions regarding his plan for uniting the English colonies under one government.

Penn married the lovely Gulielma Springett in 1672, and they spent more than a score of happy years together. The stepdaughter of Isaac Penington, Gulielma brought considerable property to her marriage from her mother's first husband, Sir William Springett, including the estate called Worminghurst in Sussex. Two years after the death of his first wife Penn married Hannah Callowhill, daughter of a wealthy Bristol merchant. She accompanied him on his second visit to Pennsylvania, and her son born in Philadelphia in 1700 was known as "John the American." Each of Penn's wives gave birth to eight children, but only two of the first family lived to maturity, and four of the second.

Because Penn placed too much trust in his business adviser, Philip Ford, he became involved in serious financial difficulties and spent a period in debtor's prison early in the eighteenth century. In 1712 William Penn suffered several strokes, which brought a loss of memory and a serious deterioration of his intellectual powers. He lived in this condition for six more years, and when he died in 1718 was buried in the grounds of Jordans Meetinghouse, northwest of London.

The People's Ancient and Just Liberties[1]

Liberty of conscience was one of the most important issues for which William Penn fought from the time he joined Quakers until the enactment of the Toleration Act in 1689. Religious intolerance was the prevailing attitude of seventeenth century Europeans whether they lived on the continent, in the British Isles, or on the other side of the Atlantic. Quakers suffered great persecution, but they were not alone, for dissenters everywhere were fined, jailed, and sometimes killed.[2]

---

[1] *The Peoples Ancient and Just Liberties Asssrted* [sic], *in the Trval of William Penn, and William Mead . . .* (n.p., 1670). This is assumed to be the first of five or six variant printings that year. Pages 10-12. It has been reprinted often since.

[2] Penn used appeals to reason, logic, and secular authority, as well as copious references to the holy scriptures, in an effort to persuade his

Early in his career, when he was only 26, Penn became involved in a court trial which vividly dramatized the case for religious and civil liberties. He and his friend, William Mead, were arrested on a Sunday morning for preaching in the street outside the Gracechurch Street meetinghouse after the authorities locked Quakers out of their building.

The trial, which was held in Old Bailey, beginning September 1, 1670, led to the landmark "Bushel case" by which the independence of juries from undue pressure by judges was confirmed once and for all. A scribe took down the proceedings in shorthand, and the printed transcript was soon being hawked on the streets as a best seller.

In the selection quoted here, Penn not only asserted the basic liberty of English citizens, he also gave evidence of a sense of humor which seldom appeared in his other writings.

Penn. We confess ourselves to be so far from recanting or declining to vindicate the assembling of ourselves to preach, pray, or worship the eternal, holy, just God, that we declare to all the world that we do believe it to be our indispensable duty to meet incessantly upon so good an account. Nor shall all the powers upon earth be able to divert us from reverencing and adoring our God who made us.

Brown. You are not here for worshiping God, but for breaking the law. You do yourselves a great deal of wrong in going on in that discourse.

Penn. I affirm I have broken no law, nor am I guilty of the indictment that is laid to my charge. And to the end that the Bench, the jury, and myself, with these that hear us, may have

---

fellow Englishmen to recognize liberty of conscience. He wrote several treatises on this subject: *The Great Case of Liberty of Conscience* (1670), *England's Present Interest Discovered* (1675), *An Address to Protestants of all Persuasions* (1679), and *A Persuasive to Moderation to Dissenting Christians* (1686).

a more direct understanding of this procedure, I desire you would let me know by what law it is you prosecute me and upon what law you ground my indictment.

Recorder. Upon the common law.

Penn. Where is that common law?

Recorder. You must not think that I am able to run up so many years, and over so many adjudged cases which we call common law to answer your curiosity.

Penn. This answer, I am sure, is very short of my question, for if it be common, it should not be so hard to produce.

Recorder. Sir, will you plead to your indictment?

Penn. Shall I plead to an indictment that hath no foundation in law? If it contain that law you say I have broken, why should you decline to produce that law, since it will be impossible for the jury to determine, or agree to bring in their verdict, who have not the law produced by which they should measure the truth of this indictment, and the guilt or contrary of my fact.

Recorder. You are a saucy fellow. Speak to the indictment.

Penn. I say it is my place to speak to matter of law. I am arraigned a prisoner; my liberty, which is next to life itself, is now concerned; you are many mouths and ears against me, and if I must not be allowed to make the best of my case, it is hard. I say again, unless you show me and the people the law you ground your indictment upon, I shall take it for granted your proceedings are merely arbitrary.

(At this time several upon the bench urged hard upon the prisoner to bear him down.)

Recorder. The question is whether you are guilty of this indictment.

Penn. The question is not whether I am guilty of this indictment, but whether this indictment be legal. It is too general and imperfect an answer to say it is the common law, unless we knew both where and what it is. For where there is no law there is no transgression, and that law which is not in being is so far from being common that it is no law at all.

Recorder. You are an impertinent fellow. Will you teach the Court what law is? It's lex non scripta, that which many have studied thirty or forty years to know, and would you have me tell you in a moment?

Penn. Certainly if the common law be so hard to be understood, it's far from being very common; but if the Lord Coke in his Institutes be of any consideration, he tells us that common law is common right, and that common right is the Great Charter privileges.

[Here Penn quoted a series of medieval laws and Sir Edward Coke.]

Recorder. Sir, you are a troublesome fellow, and it is not for the honor of the Court to suffer you to go on.

Penn. I have asked but one question, and you have not answered me, though the rights and privileges of every Englishman be concerned in it.

Recorder. If I should suffer you to ask questions till tomorrow morning, you would be never the wiser.

Penn. That is according as the answers are.

Recorder. Sir, we must not stand to hear you talk all night.

Penn. I design no affront to the Court, but to be heard in my just plea; and I must plainly tell you that if you will deny me oyer of that law which you suggest I have broken, you do at once deny me an acknowledged right and evidence to the whole world your resolution to sacrifice the privileges of Englishmen to your sinister and arbitrary designs. . . .

Mayor. Take him away, take him away; turn him into the baildock.

Penn. These are but so many vain exclamations. Is this justice or true judgment? Must I therefore be taken away because I plead for the fundamental laws of England? However, this I leave upon your consciences, who are of the jury (and my sole judges), that if these ancient fundamental laws, which relate to liberty and property, and are not limited to particular persuasions in matters of religion, must not be indispensably maintained and observed, who can say he hath right to the coat upon his back? Certainly our liberties are openly to be invaded, our wives to be ravished, our children slaved, our families ruined, and our estates led away in triumph by every sturdy beggar and malicious informer, as their trophies, but our (pretended) forfeits for conscience' sake. The Lord of heaven and earth will be judge between us in this matter.

Recorder. Be silent there.

Penn. I am not to be silent in a case wherein I am so much concerned, and not only myself but many ten thousand families besides.

Preface to the First Frame of Government[3]

This first constitution for Pennsylvania went through many drafts before William Penn decided upon the wording he would present to the settlers in his New World province. Experts have differed about the influence of various persons on this document. They have discussed the contributions of Benjamin Furly and Thomas Rudyard, and possible influence of Algernon Sidney.

The Preface, which is quoted here, undoubtedly reflects Penn's basic philosophy about the nature of government and also affirms his belief that both God and man contribute to the successful operation of government. There is more than a hint of realism in his recognition that the failings of men might lead to the downfall of government, but this quotation ends on a positive note as Penn places his faith in "men of wisdom and vir-

---

[3] *The Frame of the Government of the Province of Pennsilvania . . .* (n.p., 1682). The copy used belongs to the Historical Society of Pennsylvania. The other pamphlets consulted for these quotations are in the Quaker Collection, Haverford College Library.

tue." The Preface was omitted from the second constitution, the Charter of Liberties of 1683, and subsequent revisions.

When the great and wise God had made the world, of all his creatures it pleased Him to choose man His deputy to rule it, and to fit him for so great a charge and trust He did not only qualify him with skill and power but with integrity to use them justly. This native goodness was equally his honor and his happiness, and whilst he stood here, all went well; there was no need of coercive or compulsive means. The precept of divine love and truth in his own bosom was the guide and keeper of his innocency. But lust, prevailing against duty, made a lamentable breach upon it, and the law that before had no power over him took place upon him and his disobedient posterity, that such as would not live conformable to the holy law within should fall under the reproof and correction of the just law without in a judicial administration.

. . . The powers that be are ordained of God; whosoever therefore resisteth the power resisteth the ordinance of God. For rulers are not a terror to good works, but to evil. Wilt thou then not be afraid of the power? Do that which is good, and thou shalt have praise of the same. "He is the minister of God to thee for good. Wherefore ye must needs be subject not only for wrath but for conscience' sake. This settles the divine right of government beyond exception, and that for two ends: first, to terrify evildoers; secondly, to cherish those that do well; which gives government a life beyond corruption and makes it as durable in the world as good men shall be, so that government seems to me a part of religion itself, a thing sacred in its institution and end. For if it does not directly remove the cause, it crushes the effects of evil, and is as such . . . an emanation of the same divine Power that is both author and object of pure religion, the difference lying here, that the one is more free and mental, the other more corporal and compulsive in its operations. But that is only to evildoers, government in itself being otherwise as capable of kindness, goodness, and charity, as a more private society. They weakly err that think there is no other use for government than correction which is the coarsest part of it; daily experience tells us that the care and regulation of many other affairs more soft and daily necessary make up much the greatest part of government, and which must have followed the peopling of the world, had Adam never fell, and will continue among men on earth under the highest attainments they may arrive at by the coming of the blessed second Adam, the Lord from heaven. . . .

Governments, like clocks, go from the motion men give them, and as governments are made and moved by men, so by them they are ruined too. Wherefore governments rather depend upon men than men upon governments. Let men be good and the government can't be bad: if it be ill, they will cure it. But if men be bad, let the government be never so good, they will endeavor to warp and spoil it to their turn.

I know some say, let us have good laws, and no matter for the men that execute them; but let them consider that though good laws do well, good men do better, for good laws want good men, and be abolished or evaded by ill men, but good men will never want good laws nor suffer ill ones. 'Tis true, good laws have some awe upon ill ministers, but that is where they have not power to escape or abolish them, and the people are generally wise and good, but a loose and depraved people (which is the question) love laws and an administration like themselves. That, therefore, which makes a good constitution must keep it; viz., men of wisdom and virtue, qualities that, because they descend not with worldly inheritances, must be carefully propagated by a virtuous education of youth, for which after-ages will owe more to the care and prudence of founders and the successive magistracy than to their parents for their private patrimonies. . . .

Plan for a Union of the Colonies[4]

Penn's proposal to bring the English colonies closer together under a royal commissioner and a continental congress was first made to the Board of Trade in 1696. While Penn was in America from 1699 to 1701, he made several additional suggestions about ways to improve his plan, and visited neighboring provinces to further his ideas.

There is no means of learning whether any of the men who made proposals in the eighteenth century for uniting the colonies ever saw Penn's proposals. For this reason the importance of Penn's ideas would be overlooked if it were not for the fact that this plan is fully compatible with his proposals for Europe, and consistent with his vision regarding such things as city planning, prison reform, and the education of the young.

. . . A scheme for the general government of the Northward Plantations, which seems contrived with very good judgement; upon which account he [the author] thought it not unseasonable to offer the Heads of it here to public consideration.

1. That the colonies of Boston, Connecticut, Rhode Island, New York, both the New Jersey's, Pennsylvania, Maryland, Virginia and Carolina may be authorized to meet once a year, and oftener if need require, by their stated and appointed deputies, to debate and resolve of such measures as shall be most adviseable, at any time, to take for their public tranquillity and safety.

2. That in order to it, two persons, well qualified for understanding, sobriety and substance be appointed by each province as their representatives or deputies, which in the whole will make the Congress to consist of twenty persons.

---

[4] This first appeared in print in Charles Davenant, *Discourses on the publick revenues, and on the trade of England* . . . (2 vol.; London, 1968). Vol. II, pp. 259-261.

3. That the King's Commissioner, for that purpose specially appointed, shall have the chair and preside in the said Congress.

4. That they should meet as near as conveniently may be to the most central colony for ease of the deputies.

5. Since that may in all probability be in New York, both because it is near the center of the colonies and for that it is a frontier, and the Governor in the King's nomination, that Governor to be likewise the King's High Commissioner during the session, after the manner of Scotland.

6. That their business shall be to hear and adjust all matters of complaint or difference between province and province, as (first) where persons quit their own province and go to another that they may avoid their just debts, though able to pay them; (second) where offenders fly justice or justice cannot well be had upon such offenders in the provinces that entertain them; (third) to prevent or redress injuries in point of commerce; (fourth) to consider of ways and means to support the union and safety of these provinces against their common enemies. In which Congress the quotas of men and charges will be much easier and more equally allotted and proportioned than it is possible for any establishment made here to do, for the provinces, knowing their own condition and one another's, can debate that matter with more freedom and satisfaction and better adjust and balance their affairs in all respects for their common safety.

7. That in times of war the King's High Commissioner shall be general or chief commander of the several quotas upon service against the common enemy, as shall be thought advisable, for the good and benefit of the whole.

An Essay Towards the Peace of Europe[5]

The essay proposing that the states of Europe be united for peaceful purposes through the creation of a congress is better known today than almost any other product of Penn's fertile, creative mind.

Written by Penn in the period he withdrew from public life and was in hiding, it appeared first in 1693 while the War of the League of Augsberg was being fought. This was one of a series of wars during the reign of Louis XIV which devastated large parts of Europe and spilled over into North America. At the conclusion of the essay, Penn modestly gave credit to Henry IV of France for many of the ideas he advanced, thus perpetuating the myth that Sully's plan was the invention of that great Reformation monarch. One unusual feature of Penn's scheme was the proposal that both the Sultan of Turkey and the Czar of Russia be included in the new union.

This document, which has had an influence upon those who have prepared twentieth century constitutions for international organizations, has been quoted more fully than the others in this publication. While a few paragraphs have been omitted, all the principal points of Penn's proposal have been included.

AN ESSAY TOWARDS THE PRESENT AND FUTURE PEACE OF EUROPE (1693)

I have undertaken a subject that, I am very sensible, requires one of more sufficiency than I am master of to treat it as in truth it deserves, and the groaning state of Europe calls for; but since bunglers may stumble upon the game as well as masters, though

[5] *An Essay Towards the Present and Future Peace of Europe* (Washington D.C., 1912). This is the edition reprinted in facsimile in the Garland Library of War and Peace, along with plans of Grotius and Sully, in a volume entitled *Peace Projects of the Seventeenth Century,* eds. Blanche Cook, Charles Chatfield, and Sandi Cooper (New York, 1972).

it belongs to the skillful to hunt and catch it, I hope this essay will not be charged upon me for a fault, if it appear to be neither chimerical nor injurious, and may provoke abler pens to improve and perform the design with better judgement and success. I will say no more in excuse of myself for this undertaking but that it is the fruit of many solicitous thoughts for the peace of Europe, and they must want charity as much as the world needs quiet to be offended with me for so pacific a proposal. Let them censure my management, so they prosecute the advantage of the design; for till the millenary doctrine be accomplished, there is nothing appears to me so beneficial an expedient to the peace and happiness of this quarter of the world.

SECTION I. *Of Peace and Its Advantages*

He must not be a man but a statue of brass or stone, whose bowels do not melt when he beholds the bloody tragedies of this war in Hungary, Germany, Flanders, Ireland, and at sea; the mortality of sickly and languishing camps and navies; and the mighty prey the devouring winds and waves have made upon ships and men since '88. And as this with reason ought to affect human nature, and deeply kindred, so there is something very moving that becomes prudent men to consider, and that is the vast charge that has accompanied that blood, and which makes no mean part of these tragedies; especially if they deliberate upon the uncertainty of the war, that they know not how or when it will end, and that the expense cannot be less and the hazard is as great as before. . . .

SECTION II. *Of the Means of Peace, Which Is Justice Rather Than War*

As justice is a preserver, so it is a better procurer of peace than war. Though *pax quaeritur bello* be a usual saying, peace

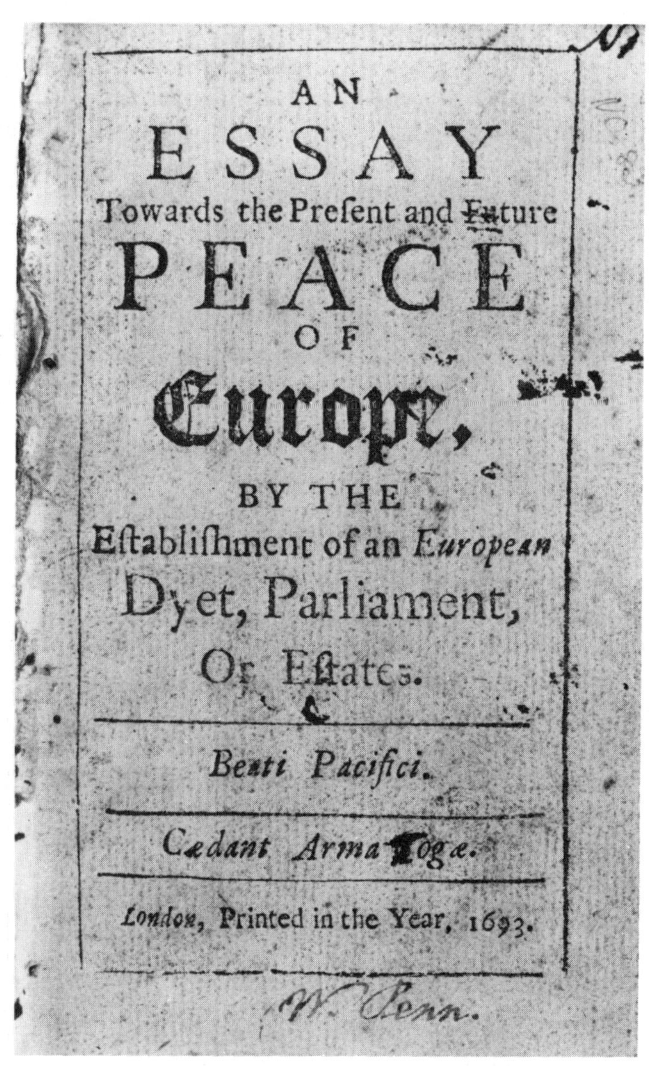

AN
ESSAY
Towards the Preſent and Future
PEACE
OF
Europe,
BY THE
Eſtabliſhment of an *European*
Dyet, Parliament,
Or Eſtates.

Beati Pacifici.

Cædant Arma Togæ.

London, Printed in the Year, 1693.

W. Penn.

Reproduction of title page of the first edition, 1693 (Only known copy.) Courtesy of Friends House Library, London. Photography R. B. Fleming.

is the end of war, and as such it was taken up by O[liver] C[romwell] for his motto, yet the use generally made of that expression shows us that, properly and truly speaking, men seek their wills by war rather than peace, and that, as they will violate it to obtain them, so they will hardly be brought to think of peace unless their appetites be some way gratified. If we look over the stories of all times, we shall find the aggressors generally moved by ambition, the pride of conquest and greatness of dominion more than right. But as those Leviathans appear rarely in the world, so I shall anon endeavor to make it evident they had never been able to devour the peace of the world and engross whole countries as they have done, if the proposal I have to make for the benefit of our present age had been then in practice.

The advantage that justice has upon war is seen by the success of embassies, that so often prevent war by hearing the pleas and memorials of justice in the hands and mouths of the wronged party. Perhaps it may be in a good degree owing to reputation or poverty or some particular interest or conveniency of princes and states as much as justice, but it is certain that, as war cannot in any sense be justified but upon wrongs received, and right, upon complaint refused, so the generality of wars have their rise from some such pretension.

This is better seen and understood at home, for that which prevents a civil war in a nation is that which may prevent it abroad, viz., justice; and we see where that is notably obstructed, war is kindled between the magistrates and people in particular kingdoms and states, which, however it may be unlawful on the side of the people, we see never fails to follow, and ought to give the same caution to princes as if it were the right of the people to do it, though I must say the remedy is almost ever worse than the disease. The agressors seldom getting what they seek, or performing, if they prevail, what they promised, and the blood and poverty that usually attend the enterprise weigh more on earth, as well as in heaven, than what they lost or suffered, or what they get by endeavoring to mend their condition comes to, which disappointment seems to be the voice of heaven and judgment of God against those violent attempts.

But to return, I say justice is the means of peace betwixt the government and the people, and [between] one man and company and another. It prevents strife and at last ends it, for besides shame or fear to contend longer, he or they, being under government, are constrained to bound their desires and resentment with the satisfaction the law gives. Thus peace is maintained by justice, which is a fruit of government, as government is from society, and society from consent.

SECTION III. *Government, Its Rise and End Under All Models*

Government is an expedient against confusion, a restraint upon all disorder; just weights and an even balance, that one man may not injure another nor himself by intemperance.

This was at first, without controversy, patrimonial; and upon the death of the father or head of the family, the eldest son or male of kin succeeded. But time breaking in upon this way of governing as the world multiplied, it fell under other claims and forms, and is as hard to trace to its original as are the copies we have of the first writings of sacred or civil matters. It is certain [that] the most natural and human is that of consent, for that binds freely, (as I may say), when men hold their liberty by their true obedience to rules of their own making. No man is judge in his own cause, which ends the confusion and blood of so many judges and executioners. For out of society every man is his own king, [and] does what he lists at his own peril. But when he comes to incorporate himself, he submits that royalty to the conveniency of the whole, from whom he receives the returns of protection, . . .

Government, then, is the prevention or cure of disorder and the means of justice, as that is of peace. For this cause they have sessions, terms, assizes, and parliaments to overrule men's passions and resentments, that they may not be judges in their own cause nor punishers of their own wrongs, which, as it is very incident to men in their corrupt state, so for that reason, they would observe no measure, nor on the other hand would any be easily reduced to their duty. Not that men know not what is right, their excesses, and wherein they are to blame, by no means; nothing is plainer to them. But so depraved is human nature that, without compulsion some way or other, too many would not readily be brought to do what they know is right and fit, or avoid what they are satisfied they should not do. . . .

SECTION IV. *Of a General Peace, or the Peace of Europe, and the Means of It*

In my first section I showed the desirableness of peace; in my next, the truest means of it, to wit, justice not war. And in my last, that this justice was the fruit of government, as government itself was the result of society, which first came from a reasonable design in men of peace. Now if the sovereign princes of Europe, who represent that society or independent state of men that was previous to the obligations of society, would, for the same reason that engaged men first into society, viz., love of peace and order, agree to meet by their stated deputies in a general diet, estates, or parliament, and there establish rules of justice for sovereign princes to observe one to another; and thus to meet yearly, or once in two or three years at farthest, or as they shall see cause, and to be styled the sovereign or imperial diet, parliament, or states of Europe; before which sovereign assembly should be brought all difference depending between one sovereign and another that cannot be made up by private embassies before the sessions begin. . . . If any of the sovereignties that constitute these imperial states shall refuse to submit their claim or pretensions to them, or to abide and perform the judgment thereof, and seek their remedy by arms or delay their compliance beyond the time prefixed in their resolutions, all the other sovereignties, united as one strength, shall compel the submission and performance of the sentence, with damages to the suffering party and charges to the sovereignties that obliged their submission. To be sure, Europe would quietly obtain the so much desired and needed peace to her harrassed inhabitants, no sovereignty in Europe having the power, and therefore cannot show the will, to dispute the conclusion; and consequently peace would be procured and continued in Europe.

SECTION V. *Of the Causes of Difference and Motives to Violate Peace*

There appears to me but three things upon which peace is broken; viz., to keep, to recover, to add. First, to keep what is one's right from the invasion of an enemy, in which I am purely defensive. Secondly, to recover, when I think myself strong enough, that which by violence I or my ancestors have lost to the arms of a stronger power, in which I am offensive. Or lastly, to increase my dominion by the acquisition of my neighbor's countries, as I find them weak and myself strong, to gratify which passion there will never want some accident or other for a pretense, and, knowing my own strength, I will be my own judge and carver. This last will find no room in the imperial states: they are an unpassable limit to that ambition. But the other two may come as soon as they please and find the justice of that sovereign court. And considering how few there are of those sons of prey, and how early they show themselves, it may be not once in an age or two, this [expedient] being established, the balance cannot well be broken.

SECTION VI. *Of Titles, Upon Which Those Differences May Arise*

But I easily foresee a question that must be answered in our way, and that is this: what is right? or else we can never know what is wrong; it is very fit that this should be established. But that is fitter for the sovereign states to resolve than me. And yet that I may lead a way to the matter, I say that title is either by a long and undoubted succession, as the crowns of Spain, France, and England; or by election, as the crown of Poland and the [Holy Roman] Empire; or by marriage, as the family of the Stuarts came by England, the elector of Brandenburg to the duchy of Cleves, and we, in ancient times, to divers places abroad; or by purchase, as hath been frequently done in Italy and Germany; or by conquest, as the Turk in Christendom, the Spaniards in Flanders, formerly mostly in the French hands, and the French in Burgundy, Normandy, Lorraine, French-County, etc. This last title is, morally speaking, only questionable. It has indeed obtained a place among the rolls of titles, but it was engrossed and recorded by the point of the sword and in bloody characters. What cannot be controlled or resisted must be submitted to, but all the world knows the date of the length of such empires and that they expire with the power of the possessor to defend them. And yet there is a little allowed to conquest too, when it has had the sanction of articles of peace to confirm it, though that hath not always extinguished the fire, but it lies, like embers and ashes, ready to kindle so soon as there is a fit matter prepared for it. Nevertheless, when conquest has been confirmed by a treaty and conclusion of peace, I must confess it is an adopted title; and if not so genuine and natural, yet, being engrafted, it is fed by that which is the security of better titles, consent. . . .

SECTION VII. *Of the Composition of These Imperial States*

The composition and proportion of this sovereign part or imperial state does, at the first look, seem to carry with it no small difficulty [about] what votes to allow for the inequality of the princes and states. But with submission to better judgments, I cannot think it invincible, for if it be possible to have an estimate of the yearly value of the several sovereign countries whose delegates are to make up this august assembly, the determination of the number of persons or votes in the states for every sovereignty will not be impracticable. Now that England, France, Spain, the Empire, etc., may be pretty exactly estimated is so plain a case, by considering the revenue of lands, the exports and entries at the Custom Houses, the books of rates and surveys that are in all governments to proportion taxes for the support of them, that the least inclination to the peace of Europe will not stand or halt at this objection.

. . . .

I suppose the Empire of Germany to send twelve; France, ten; Spain, ten; Italy, which comes to France, eight; England, six; Portugal, three; Sweden, four; Denmark, three; Poland, four; Venice, three; the seven provinces [Netherlands], four; the thirteen cantons, and little neighboring sovereignties [Switzerland], two; dukedoms of Holstein and Courland, one; and if the Turks and Muscovites are taken in, as seems but fit and just, they will make ten apiece more. The whole makes ninety. A great presence when they represent the fourth, and now the best and wealthiest, part of the known world, where religion and learning, civility and arts have their seat and empire. But it is not absolutely necessary there should be always so many persons to represent the larger sovereignties, for the votes may be given by one man of any sovereignty as well by ten or twelve; though the fuller the assembly of states is, the more solemn, effectual, and free the debates will be, and the resolutions must needs come with greater authority. The place of their first session should be central, as much as is possible; afterward as they agree.

SECTION VIII. *Of the Regulation of the Imperial States In Session*

To avoid quarrel for precedency the room may be round, and have divers doors to come in and go out at to prevent exceptions. If the whole number be cast into tens, each choosing one, they may preside by turns, to whom all speeches should be addressed, and who should collect the sense of the debates and state the question for a vote, which in my opinion, should be by ballot after the prudent and commendable method of the Venetians, which in a great degree prevents the ill effects of corruption, because if any of the delegates of those high and mighty estates could be so vile, false, and dishonorable as to be influenced by money, they have the advantage of taking their money that will give it them and of voting undiscovered to the interest of their principles and their own inclinations, as they that do understand the balloting box do very well know: A shrewd stratagem and an experimented remedy against corruption, at least [against] corrupting, for who will give their money where they may so easily be cozened, and where it is two to one they will be so; for they that will take money in such cases will not stick to lie heartily to them that give it, rather than wrong their country, when they know their lie cannot be detected.

It seems to me that nothing in this imperial parliament should pass but by three-quarters of the whole, at least seven above the balance. I am sure it helps to prevent treachery, because if money could ever be a temptation in such a court, it would cost a great deal of money to weigh down the wrong scale. All complaints should be delivered in writing in the nature of memorials, and journals kept by a proper person in a trunk or chest, which should have as many differing locks as there are tens in the states. And if there were a clerk for each ten, and a pew or table for those clerks in the assembly, and at the end of every session, one out of each ten were appointed to examine and compare the journals of those clerks and then lock them up, as I have before expressed, it would be clear and satisfactory. And each sovereignty, if they please, as is but very fit, may have an exemplification or copy of the said memorials and the journals of proceedings upon them.

The liberty and rules of speech, to be sure, they cannot fail in, who will be the wisest and noblest of each sovereignty, for its own honor and safety. If any difference can arise between those that come from the same sovereignty, that then one of the major number do give the ball[ots] of that sovereignty. I should think it extremely necessary that every sovereignty should be present under great penalties, and that none leave the session without leave till all be finished, and that neutralities in debates should by no means be endured, for any such latitude will quickly open a way to unfair proceedings and be followed by a train both of seen and unseen inconveniences. I will say little of the language in which the session of the sovereign estates should be held but, to be sure, it must be in Latin or French: the first would be very well for civilians, but the last most easy for men of quality.

SECTION IX. *Of the Objections That May Be Advanced Against the Design*

I will first give an answer to the objections that may be offered against my proposal, and in my next and last section I shall endeavor to show some of the manifold conveniences that would follow this European league or confederacy.

The first of them is this, that the strongest and richest sovereignty will never agree to it, and if it should, there would be danger of corruption more than of force [at] one time or other. I answer to the first part, he is not stronger than all the rest, and for that reason you should promote this and compel him into it, especially before he be so, for then it will be too late to deal with such a one. To the last part of the objection I say the way is as open now as then and it may be the number fewer and as easily come at. However, if men of sense and honor and substance are chosen, they will either scorn the baseness or have wherewith to pay for the knavery; at least they may be watched so, that one may be a check upon the other, and all prudently limited by the sovereignty they represent. In all great points, especially before a final resolve, they may be obliged to transmit to their principles the merits of such important cases depending, and receive their last instruction, which may be done in four and twenty days at the most, as the place of their session may be appointed.

The second is, that it will endanger an effeminacy by such a disuse of the trade of soldiery, that if there should be any need for it upon any occasion, we should be at a loss, as they were in Holland in '72.

There can be no danger of effeminacy, because each sovereignty may introduce as temperate or severe a discipline in the education of youth as they please by low living and due labor. Instruct them in mechanical knowledge and in natural philosophy by operation, which is the honor of the German nobility. This would make them men, neither women nor lions, for soldiers are t'other extreme to effeminacy. But the knowledge of nature and the useful as well as agreeable operations of art give men an understanding of themselves, of the world they are born into, how to be useful and serviceable, both to themselves and others, and how to save and help, not injure or destroy. The knowledge of government in general, the particular constitutions of Europe, and, above all, of his own country are very recommending accomplishments. This fits him for the parliament and council at home, and the courts of princes and services in the imperial states abroad. At least, he is a good commonwealths-man and can be useful to the public or retire, as there may be occasion.

To the other part of the objection, of being at a loss for soldiery as they were in Holland in '72, the proposal answers for itself. One has war no more than the other, and will be as much to seek upon occasion. Nor is it to be thought that anyone will keep up such an army after such an empire is on foot, which may hazard the safety of the rest. However, if it be seen requisite, the question may be asked by order of the sovereign states, why such a one either raises or keeps up a formidable body of troops, and he obliged forthwith to reform or reduce them, lest anyone, by keeping up a great body of troops, should surprise a neighbor. But a small force in every other sovereignty, as it is capable or accustomed to maintain, will certainly prevent that danger and vanquish any such fear.

The third objection is that there will be great want of employment for younger brothers of families, and that the poor must either turn soldiers or thieves. I have answered that in my return to the second objection. We shall have the more merchants and husbandmen, or ingenious naturalists, if the government be but anything solicitous of the education of their youth, which, next to the present and immediate happiness of any country, ought of all things to be the care and skill of the government. For such as the youth of any country is bred, such is the next generation, and the government in good or bad hands.

I am come now to the last objection, that sovereign princes and states will hereby become not sovereign, a thing they will never endure. But this also, under correction, is a mistake, for they remain as sovereign at home as ever they were. Neither their power over their people nor the usual revenue they pay them is diminished; it may be the war establishment may be reduced, which will indeed of course follow, or be better employed to the advantage of the public. So that the sovereignties are as they were, for none of them have now any sovereignty over one another; and if this be called a lessening of their power, it must be only because the great fish can no longer eat up the little ones, and that each sovereignty is equally defended from injuries and disabled from committing them. "Cedant arma togae" [Let wars yield to peace] is a glorious sentence; the voice of the dove, the olive branch of peace, a blessing so great that when it pleases God to chastise us severely for our sins, it is with the rod of war that, for the most part, He whips us, and experience tells us none leaves deeper marks behind it.

SECTION X. *Of the Real Benefits That Flow from This Proposal About Peace*

I am come to my last section, in which I shall enumerate some of those many real benefits that flow from this proposal for the present and future peace of Europe.

Let it not, I pray, be the least that it prevents the spilling of so much human and Christian blood, for a thing so offensive to God, and terrible and afflicting to men, as that has ever been must recommend our expedient beyond all objections. For what can a man give in exchange for his life as well as [his] soul? And though the chiefest in government are seldom personally exposed, yet it is a duty incumbent upon them to be tender of the lives of their people, since without all doubt they are accountable to God for the blood that is spilt in their service. So that besides the loss of so many lives, of importance to any government, both for labor and propagation, the cries of so many widows, parents, and fatherless are prevented, that cannot be very pleasant in the ears of any government, and is the natural consequence of war in all government.

There is another manifest benefit which redounds to Christendom by this peaceable expedient: the reputation of Christianity will in some degree be recovered in the sight of infidels; which, by the many bloody and unjust wars of Christians, not only with them, but one with another, hath been greatly impaired. For, to the scandal of that holy profession, Christians that glory in their Saviour's name have long devoted the credit and dignity of it to their worldly passions as often as they have been excited by the impulses of ambition or revenge. . . .

Nor is this all the advantage that follows to sovereignties upon this head of money and good husbandry, to whose service and happiness this short discourse is dedicated, for it saves the great expense that frequent and splendid embassies require and all their appendages of spies and intelligence, which in the most prudent governments have devoured mighty sums of money, and that not without some immoral practices also, such as corrupting of servants to betray their masters by revealing their secrets —not to be defended by Christian or old Roman virtues. But here, where there is nothing to fear, there is little to know, and therefore the purchase is either cheap or may be wholly spared. I might mention pensions to the widows and orphans of such as die in wars and of those that have been disabled in them, which rise high in the revenue of some countries.

Our fourth advantage is that the towns, cities, and countries that might be laid waste by the rage of war are thereby preserved, a blessing that would be very well understood in Flanders and Hungary and indeed upon all the borders of sovereignties, where are almost ever the stages of spoil and misery, of which the stories of England and Scotland do sufficiently inform us without looking over the water.

The fifth benefit of this peace is the ease and security of travel and traffic, a happiness never understood since the Roman Empire has been broken into so many sovereignties. But we may easily conceive the comfort and advantage of traveling through the governments of Europe by a pass from any of the sovereignties of it, which this league and state of peace will naturally make authentic . . . And for the same reason why no Christian monarch will adventure to oppose or break such a union, the Grand Seignior [Sultan of Turkey] will find himself obliged to concur for the security of what he holds in Europe, where, with all his strength, he would feel it an overmatch for him. The prayers, tears, treason, blood, and devastation that war has cost in Christendom for these two last ages especially must add to the credit of our proposal and the blessing of the peace thereby humbly recommended.

The seventh advantage of a European imperial diet, parliament, or estates is that it will beget and increase personal friendship between princes and states, which tends to the rooting up of wars and planting peace in a deep and fruitful soil. For princes have the curiosity of seeing the courts and cities of other countries as well as private men, if they could as securely and familiarly gratify their inclinations. It were a great motive to the tranquillity of the world that they could freely converse face to face and personally and reciprocally give and receive marks of civility and kindness.

. . . .

To conclude this section, there is yet another manifest privilege that follows this intercourse and good understanding, which methinks should be very moving with princes; viz., that hereby they may choose wives for themselves, such as they love, and not by proxy merely to gratify interest, an ignoble motive, and that rarely begets or continues that kindness which ought to be between men and their wives—a satisfaction very few princes ever knew and to which all other pleasures ought to resign. Which has often obliged me to think that the advantage of private men upon princes by family comforts is a sufficient balance against their great power and glory; the one being more in imagination than real, and often unlawful, but the other natural, solid, and commendable. Besides, it is certain, parents' loving well before they are married, which very rarely happens to princes, has kind and generous influences upon their offspring, which, with their example, makes them the better husbands and wives in their turn. This in great measure prevents unlawful love and the mischiefs of those intrigues that are wont to follow them: what hatred, feuds, wars, and desolations have in divers ages flowed from unkindness between princes and their wives? What unnatural divisions among their children and ruin to their families, if not loss of their countries by it? . . .

THE CONCLUSION

I will conclude this my proposal of a European sovereign or imperial diet, parliament, or estates with that which I have touched upon before, and which falls under the notice of everyone concerned, by coming home to their particular and respective experience within their own sovereignties, that the same rules of justice and prudence by which parents and masters govern their families, and magistrates their cities, and estates their republics, and princes and kings their principalities and kingdoms, Europe may obtain and preserve peace among her sovereignties. For wars are the duels of princes; and as government in kingdoms and states prevents men being judges and executioners for themselves, overrules private passions as to injuries or revenge, and subjects the great as well as the small to the rule of justice, that power might not vanquish or oppress right, nor one neighbor act an independency and sovereignty upon another, while they have resigned that original claim to the benefit and comfort of society; so this being soberly weighed in the whole and parts of it, it will not be hard to conceive or frame nor yet to execute the design I have here proposed.

. . . .

But I confess I have the passion to wish heartily that the honor of proposing and effecting so great and good a design might be owing to England of all the countries in Europe, as something of the nature of our expedient was, in design and preparation, to the wisdom, justice, and valor of Henry the Fourth of France, whose superior qualities, raising his character above those of his ancestors or contemporaries, deservedly gave him the style of Henry the Great. For he was upon obliging the princes and estates of Europe to a politic balance, when the Spanish faction for that reason contrived and accomplished his murder by the hands of Ravaillac. I will not then fear to be censured for proposing an expedient for the present and future peace of Europe when it was not only the design but glory of one of the greatest princes that ever reigned in it, and is found practicable in the constitution of one of the wisest and powerfullest states of it. So that to conclude, I have very little to deserve, for this great king's example tells us it is fit to be done, and Sir William Temple's History shows us by a surpassing instance that it may be done, and Europe by her incomparable miseries makes it now necessary to be done, that my share is only thinking of it at this juncture, and putting it into the common light for the peace and prosperity of Europe.

Appendix

It has been estimated that William Penn published one and one-half million words, in some 150 titles during his lifetime. A substantial portion of his writings were edited by Joseph Besse and published in a handsome two volume folio edition under the title *A Collection of the Works of William Penn . . .* (London, 1726). Three more editions of his writings appeared in the next century, and in 1974 the first edition was republished by the AMS Press. A number of separate titles have also been reprinted: notably *Some Fruits of Solitude,* the *Essay Towards . . . the Peace of Europe,* and *No Cross, No Crown,* all mentioned earlier. Over the years various collections of selections have been published. The latest, and unquestionably the most useful, was prepared by Frederick B. Tolles and E. Gordòn Alderfer in 1957 under the title, *The Witness of William Penn.* This volume is out of print, but an effort is being made to bring out a new edition.

The quality of Penn's writing varied considerably from title to title. Sometimes he wrote with a grace which delighted the reader, as in the aphorisms in *Some Fruits of Solitude,* or his *Letter to the Free Society of Traders* (1683), in which he described the aborigines in Pennsylvania. At other times he allowed himself to be caught up in piling fact on fact, and authority on authority to the point where he exhausted his reader. The essays he wrote in a hurry, without taking time to go over them to correct, prune, and improve are the least impressive. His best writing was often done while he was in prison, or during his enforced withdrawal from society after the Revolution of 1688. He published steadily for thirty-five years after he joined Friends, but wrote comparatively little after *More Fruits of Solitude* appeared in 1702. One of the selections quoted here was written in 1670, two in the 1690's, and the fourth in 1682. A comprehensive, though not definitive list of his works may be found in Catherine Owens Peare, *William Penn* (Philadelphia, 1957; paper, Ann Arbor, Mich., 1966).

While the selections printed here are taken from the earliest sources available in most cases, the spelling, capitalization, and punctuation has been modernized. Where portions are omitted, this is indicated by elision points (. . .). In the few cases where additional words have been inserted, this is indicated by brackets ([]).

SUGGESTIONS FOR FURTHER READING

Beatty, Edward C. O., *William Penn as Social Philosopher* (New York, 1939).

Brailsford, Mabel R., *The Making of William Penn* (New York, 1930).

Bronner, Edwin B., *William Penn's "Holy Experiment"* (New York, 1962).

Buranelli, Vincent, *The King and the Quaker* (Philadelphia, 1962).

Comfort, William W., *William Penn, 1644-1718* (Philadelphia, 1944).

Dunn, Mary Maples, *William Penn, Politics and Conscience* (Princeton, 1967).

Endy, Melvin B., Jr., *William Penn and Early Quakerism* (Princeton, 1973).

Hull, William I., *William Penn, a Topical Biography* (New York, 1937).

Illick, Joseph E., *William Penn the Politician* (Ithaca, N.Y., 1965).

Wildes, Harry E., *William Penn* (New York, 1974).